S0-BBP-512

# JESUS PLAYS
## FOR PRIMARY GRADES

## by
# Dorinda Clark

## Illustrated by Maryann Read

# In Appreciation

To Judy Turk, Coordinator of CCD and all religion classes for St. Veronica Parish in Milwaukee.

In her gentle manner she never permitted me to forget a promise made to write, for publication, the little plays I had written for use in religion classes for children.

Thanks, Judy. But for your persistence and encouragement, they might never have been written.

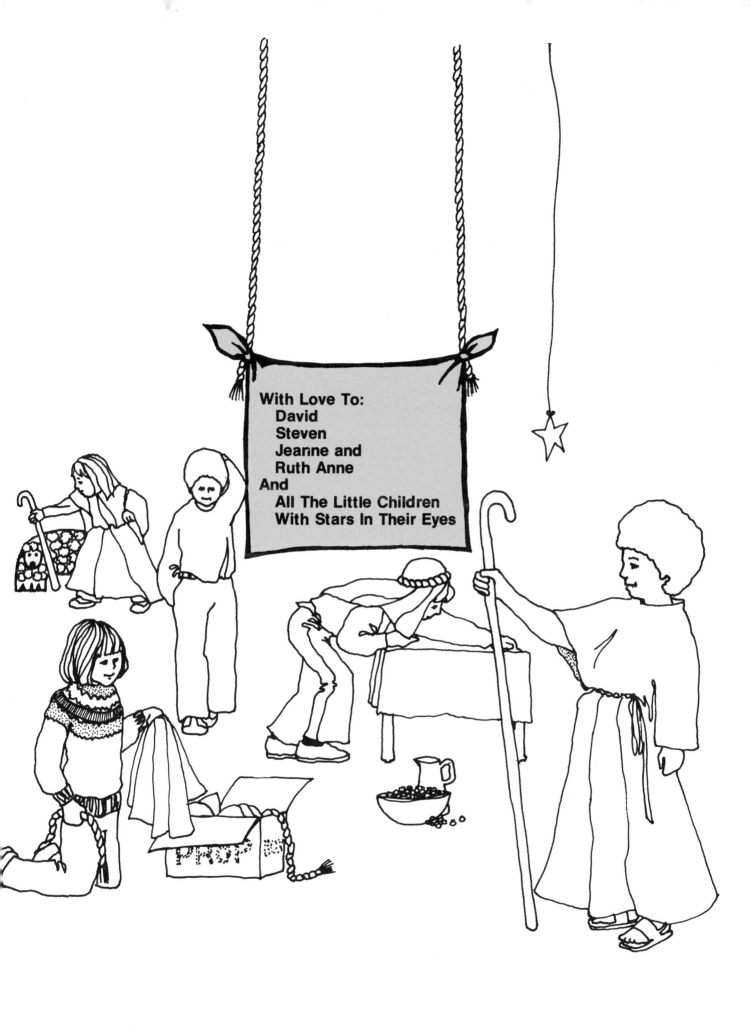

With Love To:
    David
    Steven
    Jeanne and
    Ruth Anne
And
    All The Little Children
    With Stars In Their Eyes

© Copyright 1978 by Dorinda Clark. All rights reserved. No part of this book should be reproduced by any means except for purposes of review without permission from the publisher. For such permission address Twenty-Third Publications, P.O. Box 180, West Mystic, CT 06388.

Library of Congress Catalog Card Number 77-83984

ISBN 0-89622-084-2

Printed in the United States of America by Abbey Press, St. Meinrad, Indiana

# CONTENTS

# Plays

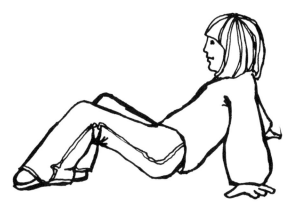

# ABOUT THESE PLAYS

These little plays were written primarily for children in grades one through four, and arranged for classroom use in teaching the message of Jesus.

They are intended to be used in addition to, or as a change of pace from, formal textbooks. Since play acting is always enjoyable for children, it is hoped that in this pleasant association the scriptural lessons will be retained for life.

Plays may be produced spontaneously, as a lesson, using a few classroom articles as props, especially where time and space are limited and scenery and costumes are not available. Children have great imaginations, and love the make-believe aspect of substitute props. They easily can visualize a scene without real "scenery."

Dialogue purposely has been kept simple and in short sentence form to facilitate easy understanding and repetition.

The fact that these plays are aimed particularly for use with primary grades, does not preclude their use with older children who are able to memorize lines and perform before an audience.

Plays are designed for full class participation so that no child might feel left out or rejected.

The usual "Curtain Rise" in plays has been omitted and Narrator substituted. (See paragraph 4 of Aids for Classroom Use.)

# AIDS FOR CLASSROOM USE

1. Before acting out each play, it is advisable to read the related bible story to the children, and to locate the message or moral through discussion.
2. Select the main characters and go over the dialogue with them.
3. **Setting:** (a) Set up the props and inform the children what each object represents; i.e., a chair may be a rock, a tree, etc.

   (b) If two scenes are required, set these up in opposite corners of the room.

4. **Narrator:** Usually a teacher acts as the storyteller to appeal to the senses and imagination of the children in
   a) describing the scene,
   b) directing the action,
   c) assigning roles to children,
   d) Since primary children are too young for extensive memorization, Narrator will read each line, indicating the name of the character who speaks it. The child selected to play that role will simply repeat his lines after the Narrator. For example:

Narrator: Jesus says, "It is getting late. . . ." The child taking the role of Jesus, repeats the line. Narrator then reads the next line (Peter's): "Yes, Jesus, it has been a tiring day." Child playing role of Peter repeats his or her line, etc.

This practice has never seemed to dampen the children's enthusiasm for acting. It does, however, require patience by the Narrator to keep the learning atmosphere calm and enjoyable.

Older children may be permitted to ad-lib some lines.

5. Although the plays are intended as class exercises, produced simply without costumes or props, these may be used.
6. If there are discrepancies between the numbers of boys and girls and the male and female roles, use diplomacy in leading children to play the parts of the opposite sex.
7. Songs and records listed are suggestions selected to carry through the theme for each play. Many other songs and hymns are also suitable.

# PLAY I

## Angels Announce Jesu

### LUKE 2:8-20

**SHEEP PROP**

USE GLUE TO STICK COTTON BALLS ON CARDBOARD CUT-OUT

GLUE

MARKER

USE HEAVY SHEARS OR A MAT KNIFE TO CUT OUT SHEEP CUT STRIP + PASTE ON BACK TO MAKE SHEEP STAND

USE WIDE-TIP MARKER TO DRAW OUTLINES AND DETAIL

**ANGEL COSTUME**

WAISTBAND

FOLDED TWIN SIZE SHEET* CUT IN HALF

NECK HOLE CUT IN FOLD OF SHEET

*HAVE CHILDREN COLOR SHEETS WITH CRAYONS - STARS + FLOWERS OR ABSTRACT DESIGNS

CUT LINE

**STAR PROP**

CARDBOARD

FOIL WRAP

FOIL

## Play Season:

Use during Advent or Christmas season. Explain that God sent His son Jesus to redeem us so that we might all go to heaven when we die.

## Props and Production:

**Scene I. Shepherds in field.** Darken room to simulate night.

**Campfire.** Crushed red cellophane over wire covered bulb on extension cord. Pieces of wood placed around the edge. Or crushed red and brown burlap or cloth without light bulb. (Be careful of hot bulbs.)

**Sheep.** Cardboard cut-out sheep may be placed in background, or sheep from a plywood outdoor Christmas display, if available. Spotlight if possible.

**Brighten scene as Angels arrive.** For variation, only the announcing Angel may be seen. Angels' song may come from record behind screen.

**Scene II. Mark off area and designate as stable by Narrator.**

**Christ Child.** A baby doll, preferred to child. Less distraction.

**Manger.** Cardboard box, cut low. May use child and manger from large Nativity scene, if available.

**Mary and Joseph may wear scarves loosely over their heads.**

**Shepherds' crooks.** Canes, broom handles, sticks, etc.

**Star.** Large cardboard cut-out covered with aluminum foil. Place above or near stable.

**Gift.** Toy lamb preferred. A wrapped gift may be substituted, if no lamb is available. Dialogue may be changed accordingly.

# Birth To Shepherds

**Note:** As an Advent activity, children may be involved in preparing props for the play. *Angel's robe:* **Wide strip of white sheet cut to length, with hole cut for head and tied around waist with narrow strip. The manger:** A cardboard box may be covered or decorated. **Star:** Cardboard cut-out covered with foil, shiny side out. **Sheep:** Draw forms on cardboard and cut out.

## Songs and Music:

### Suggested Songs:

Scene I—Background music: O Little Town of Bethlehem. Angels sing: Hark the Herald Angels Sing. Any Christmas record.
Scene II—Finale: Silent Night, or O Come All You Faithful.

# BLOOPER

**While presenting the Angels Announce Jesus' Birth, one of the children asked:**

**"Why don't you let some kids play the three wise guys?" (Magi).**

# PLAY I

## Angels Announce Jesu[s]
### LUKE 2:8-20

## Script

### Characters

Infant Jesus
Mary
Joseph
Angels (Any number)
Shepherds ( " " )

### Scene I

**Time:** Early Christmas morning.

**Scene:** A field near Bethlehem. Shepherds recline around a campfire, watching their sheep. Soft music in the background. *(See Production Notes, etc.)*

**Narrator:** It is early in the morning of Christmas day. It is still dark and everything is peaceful. Shepherds are resting but keeping watch over their sheep. Suddenly it gets bright as day.

**Angel** *(Appearing):* Do not be afraid. I bring you good news. Today a Savior has been born.

**Other Angels** *(Appear singing):* Hark the Herald Angels Sing. *(After song, they leave scene. First Angel remains.) (Shepherds sit up.)*

**First Shepherd:** Did you hear that?

**Second Shepherd:** Yes, but I thought it was a dream.

**Third Shepherd:** It was so beautiful. It must have been Angels.

# Birth To Shepherds

**First Shepherd** *(Jumping to his feet):* They were singing about a newborn King.

**Second Shepherd** *(Excitedly):* The Savior is born! Let's go find him! *(Stands up.)*

**Third Shepherd:** But how can we find him? *(Gets up slowly.)*

**Angel:** He was born in a stable. A bright star will lead you. *(Angel leaves Scene.)*

**First Shepherd** *(Pointing)* Look! There's the star! Let's follow it. *(They exit.)*

### Scene II

**Scene:** Inside the stable. Mary and Joseph are kneeling on either side of the child who rests in a manger. *(See Production Notes.)*

**Narrator:** This is the stable in which Jesus was born. Mary and Joseph kneel beside the manger. In the distance is the sound of shepherds approaching.

**Joseph:** Listen, Mary, do you hear voices? Someone is coming.

**Mary:** Yes, I hear them. Maybe they come to see Jesus. *(Enter Shepherds. They stand for a while, silently, looking at the child. One Shepherd holds a little lamb. He moves forward shows it to the Christ Child, then sets it on the floor near the manger.)*

**Shepherd:** Little Savior, we bring you a gift. It is our best little lamb. *(Shepherds kneel.)*

End.

# PLAY 2 Jesus Loves Little Ch
### LUKE 18:15-17

JESUS' ROBE

HAVE CHILDREN COLOR ROBE WITH FLOWERS & STRIPES

BELT CUT FROM END OF SHEET

## Play Season:

To follow discussion on Jesus' love for children. Even though he was tired, he called them to come to him and blessed them.

## Props and Production:

Cardboard box or overturned chair may simulate the mound against which Jesus leans. No other props needed.

## Songs and Music:

Jesus Loves the Little Children—*Reader's Digest Family Songbook of Faith and Joy.*

en

# Script

## Characters

Jesus
Disciples * Peter
James
John
**Parents and Children (Any number)**

**Time:** Early evening.

**Setting:** An open field.

**Narrator:** It is evening. Jesus and his disciples are resting after a day of teaching. Jesus is reclining against a mound. His disciples sit around him, talking softly. Standing at a distance from them is a group of parents and children looking toward Jesus.

**Jesus** *(Wiping his brow):* It is getting late, but let's rest here awhile before we go on.

**Peter** *(Sighing):* Yes, Jesus, it has been a tiring day.

**Parent** *(Pointing to Jesus):* Look! there's Jesus. Let's ask him to bless our children.

*(Group moves a few steps toward Jesus, then stops.)*

**Peter:** Stop! Do not come here. Jesus is resting.

**James:** He has been teaching all day. He is tired.

**John:** Please go away. Come back another day.

**Jesus** *(Rising to his feet and frowning at the disciples):* Why do you send them away? Let the little ones come to me, for of such is the Kingdom of God.
*(Group moves slowly toward Jesus)*

**Jesus** *(Extending his arms toward them):* Come to me, little ones. I will bless you. *(He lays his hands on the children's heads and looks up to heaven.)*

**Disciples** *(Smiling to one another):* Jesus really does love little children.

End

# PLAY 3

## Jesus Calms the Storm
### LUKE 8:22-25

### Play Season:

After a discussion on trust in the Lord. When Jesus is with us we need have no fear.

### Props and Production:

Substituting for the boat may be an area rug, a large mat, small chairs placed side by side in an oval shape, or even a chalk mark on the floor.

Howling wind and thunder sounds may be made by class members not in the boat. Jesus and disciples sway to simulate rocking motion of the boat in the high waves. Swaying is stopped to indicate calm.

### Songs and Music:

Song: Put Your Hand in the Hand of the Man Who Stilled the Waters. Words and Music by Gene MacLellan—Pg. 173, *Reader's Digest Family Songbook of Faith and Joy*. Recording (45) OCEAN, (group) by Kamasutra No. 519. Also, many albums by major stars, including Engelbert Humperdink, Dick Hyman, Bing Crosby and Joan Baez.

# Script

## Characters

**Jesus**
**Disciples (12)**

**Time:** Late afternoon.

**Setting:** Jesus and disciples in a boat, crossing a lake. A storm is brewing. *(See Production Notes.)*

**Narrator:** Jesus and his disciples are crossing a lake. It is beginning to storm. Jesus has been teaching all day and is tired. He has fallen asleep. The boat begins to rock in the high waves, and thunder is heard. The wind howls. *(See Production Notes.)*

**First Disciple:** The storm is growing worse. Waves are splashing into the boat.

**Second Disciple:** The boat will fill with water and we will drown.

**Third Disciple:** Look! *(Pointing to Jesus)* Jesus is asleep. *(They all look at Jesus who is sleeping, his head resting on his arm.)*

**Disciples 2(Together):** Jesus! Jesus! Wake up. *(Jesus continues to sleep.)*

**Disciples** *(Shouting louder):* Jesus! Master! Wake up or we will all drown. Save us!

**Jesus** *(Awakens slowly and looks at them. He raises his arms over the water):* Wind you will stop! Water be calm! *(Swaying stops to indicate calm. Wind and thunder stop.)*

**Jesus:** *(To disciples):* Where is your faith in me? Did you think I would let you drown?

**Disciples** *(to one another):* Who is this man who can make the wind and the water obey him? Surely he must be the son of God.

End

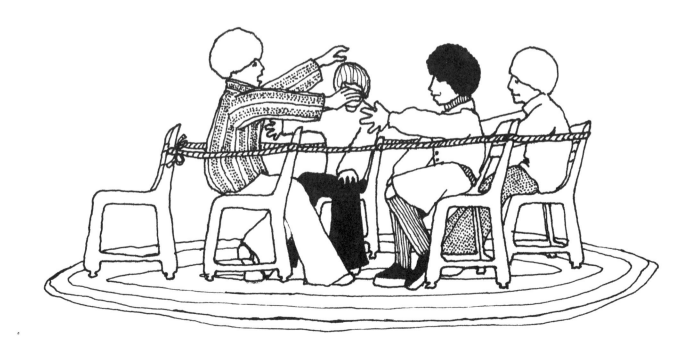

# PLAY 4

## Zacchaeus

LUKE 19:1-10

### Play Season:

May be used in preparation for sacrament of Penance. Illustrates that Jesus loves and forgives sinners. Zacchaeus repents.

### Props and Production:

**Street Scene.** Tree may be any solid object. A chair (not folding) a ladder, or a solid box. Any object to raise Zacchaeus above the heads of crowd. Choose smallest boy in class for Zacchaeus.

### Songs and Music:

Zacchaeus, from record Joy Is Like the Rain, by Medical Mission Sisters.
Christ Light, Album: RUN, COME, SEE, by Robert Blue. F.E.L.
Record Release. S-272.

# Script

## Characters

**Jesus**
**Zacchaeus**
**Disciples (2 or 3)**
**People of the Town**

**Time:** Morning.
**Scene:** A street in Jericho.
**Narrator:** Jesus and his disciples walk slowly along the street in Jericho. A crowd of people gather around them. All are anxious to see Jesus. They have heard of his miracles.
**Zacchaeus** *(Rushes up, tries to see Jesus, but cannot see over the heads of the crowd):* I can't even see him. I know what I'll do, I'll climb up a tree. (Runs ahead and climbs tree.) *(See Production Notes.)*
**People:** We have come to see you, Jesus. We have heard about the wonderful things you have done. (Or ad lib.)

*(Jesus and crowd move forward and stop near tree.)*
**Jesus** *(Looking up into tree):* Zacchaeus, what are you doing in that tree?
**Zacchaeus:** I wanted to see you, Jesus, and I'm so short I can't see over their heads.
**Jesus:** Come down, Zacchaeus, I want to talk with you. *(Zacchaeus descends and stands near Jesus.)*
**Jesus:** Zacchaeus, you will see me again later today. May I come to your house for dinner? *(Zacchaeus looks happy. Claps hands.)*

**People** *(Look angry. Begin to grumble):* Why should Jesus go to his house? Zacchaeus is not an honest man. He cheats us.
**Zacchaeus** *(Stops rejoicing and looks serious.):* I'm sorry, Jesus.
**Narrator:** Zacchaeus sees that the people think Jesus should not visit him. He realizes that if he wants Jesus to come to his home, he must be a better man.
**Zacchaeus:** Jesus, I am going to change my life. I will give half of everything I have to the poor. If I have cheated anyone, I will pay him back in full.
*(People quiet down and look at Jesus.)*
**Jesus:** Zacchaeus, you are forgiven. Salvation has come to your house today.

End

## Marriage Feast at C

### JOHN 2:1-10

### Play Season:

Has Eucharistic signification. Also shows Jesus' love for people. He performs a miracle to save his friend from the embarrassment of running out of wine at the feast.

### Props and Production:

**Banquet table.** Any long table or several smaller tables placed together. If tables are unavailable, a long sheet of white shelf paper placed on the floor may serve. Children sit around it picnic fashion.

**A small table, chair, or stool** near the banquet table holds two opaque water jugs (or pitchers). Opaque is specified so that, as waiters take them from the room to add the fruit drink, the color of the drink may not be seen when servants/waiters return with the "water."

For identification, bride wears **a white scarf** as a veil and groom wears a **boutonniere.** They sit at center of table.

Jesus and Mary sit at end of table, to facilitate their leaving table to speak to waiters.

**On table.** A paper cup at each place, with a small amount of fruit juice in each cup. To avoid spillage (not 100% effective) more drink is added later. Cookies, crackers or other food on plates on the table. (Be prepared, as it disappears quickly. No miracle.)

### Songs and Music:

Peace, Joy and Happiness, Album: HAND IN HAND, by Joe Wise. World Library of Sacred Music.

Gathered together in Love, Album: SONGS FOR YOUNG CHILDREN by Mary Lou Walker. Paulist Press.

PROPS

CARDBOARD BOUTONNIERE (GROOM)
ALSO CUT AND COLOR ONE FLOWER FOR EACH GUEST

← WHITE SCARF OR PIECE OF SHEET (BRIDE)

OPAGUE PITCHER

PAPER CUPS →

# Script

## Characters

**Jesus**
**Disciples (2)**
**Mary**
**Bride**
**Bridegroom**
**Chief Steward**
**Waiter**
**Guests (Any number)**

**Time:** Wedding day

**Scene:** Diningroom of bride's home (See Production Notes, etc.)

**Narrator:** It is the wedding day. The bride and groom are seated at a large table. Jesus and Mary are guests. They sit near the end of the table. The chief steward and waiters stand a short distance away at a small table on which are two jugs *(pitchers)*. A small amount of wine has been poured into each cup for the toast. Disciples and guests are also present.

**First Guest** *(Rises):* Let's drink a toast to the bride and groom. *(Lifts his cup. Others do the same.)*

**All Guests:** To their health and happiness.

**Mary** *(To Jesus):* Son, they do not have enough wine.

**Jesus** *(To Mary):* What would you have me do?

**Mary** *(Leaves the table to talk to chief steward):* Whatever Jesus asks you to do, please do it. *(She returns to her place at the table.)*

**Jesus** *(Leaves table and goes over to chief steward):* Will you please ask your servants to fill the jugs with water? *(Jesus remains standing to await their return.)*

**Chief Steward** *(To servers):* Do as Jesus has asked. *(Servers pick up jugs and leave the room. They add the fruit drink, return to room and place jugs on the table.)*

**Jesus** *(Extending hands over jugs, looks up to heaven and says a silent prayer, then turns to the waiters):* Pour some out and take it to the chief steward to taste. *(Waiters do this.)*

**Chief Steward:** Where did you get this wine? It is better than the first you served.

**Waiter:** Jesus blessed the water and changed it into wine. *(Waiters pour wine into guests' cups.)*

**Guests:** This wine is the best we have ever tasted. Jesus has performed a miracle. A miracle! A miracle!

End

# PLAY 6

## Jesus Cures the Dea

MARK 7:31-37

### Play Season:

May follow discussion of faith, as deaf man showed faith in Jesus to heal him. Also, general use.

### Props and Production:

Street scene. No props. Corner of classroom or aisle.

### Songs and Music:

"Thank you Hymn" from Album: RUN, COME, SEE, by Robert Blue—F.E.L. Record Release

"Shout out the Good News," Album: SEASONS by Medical Mission Sisters.

Man

# Script

## Characters

Jesus
Disciples—Peter and Andrew
Deaf Man
Friends (2)

**Scene:** Near Sea of Galilee. Jesus and disciples walk along.

**Narrator:** Jesus, Peter and Andrew are walking in Galilee. Three men approach them. The man in center is being led by the others, as they approach Jesus.

**First Friend:** Jesus, will you please help him?

**Jesus** *(To man being led):* How can I help you? *(Man makes signs using his fingers. Points to ears.)*

**Second Friend:** He cannot hear or speak. Can you cure him?

**First Friend:** We have heard how you have cured others. *(Deaf man looks anxiously at Jesus.)*

**Jesus** *(Taking deaf man's arm):* Come. *(They walk a few steps then stop. Jesus puts his hands over the deaf man's ears, then touches his lips):* Be opened!

**Deaf Man** *(Looking happy):* I can hear! I can speak! Thank you Jesus, thank you.

End

# PLAY 7

## Jesus Feeds the Mult

### JOHN 6:1-15

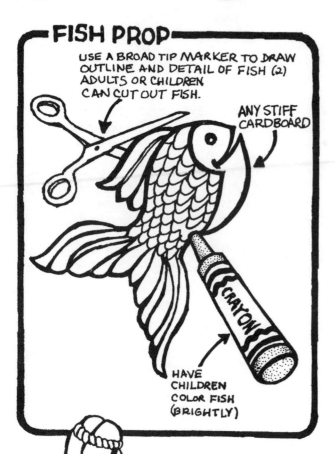

**FISH PROP**

USE A BROAD TIP MARKER TO DRAW OUTLINE AND DETAIL OF FISH (2) ADULTS OR CHILDREN CAN CUT OUT FISH.

ANY STIFF CARDBOARD

HAVE CHILDREN COLOR FISH (BRIGHTLY)

CRAYON

## Play Season:

General use. But also after a discussion of the world's poor and hungry. Jesus shows compassion for the hungry. Jesus shared—when you share you receive more than you give.

## Props and Production:

**A small basket for fish.**
**Fish.** 2 cardboard cut-outs.
**Five small loaves of bread or rolls**
**Another small basket** for the five loaves of bread, or rolls. **Several waste paper baskets** for crumbs. (Crumbs are imaginary, bread usually disappears completely.)

## Songs and Music:

"O Bread of Life," *People's Mass Book.* 3rd (Voice) Ed. World Library Publications.
"Thank you Lord," Album HI GOD, North American Liturgy Resources.

# Script

## Characters

**Jesus**
**Disciples—Philip**
        **Andrew**
**Woman**
**Boy**
**Crowd**

**Time:** Late afternoon
**Scene:** An open field near Tiberias. Jesus and disciples stand. People are seated on the ground.
**Narrator:** It is getting late. Jesus has been teaching the people all day and everyone is weary and hungry.
**Philip:** Jesus, it is getting late. These people have not eaten all day. Shall we send them home for their meal?
**Jesus:** Some have come a long way. We should feed them.
**Philip:** But Jesus, we do not have enough food, or money to buy it.
**Jesus** *(To crowd):* Do you have any food with you?
**Woman:** I have five small loaves.
**Boy:** I have two little fish.
**Andrew:** That is not enough to feed so many.
**Jesus:** Bring the food to me. *(Disciples take a small basket and pick up the food and bring it to Jesus.)*

**Jesus** *(Takes basket, blesses the food, breaks the bread, and gives it to Andrew):* Here, give this to the people. Let them eat. *(Andrew passes the basket, each person takes food.)*
**Jesus:** After they have eaten, gather up the crumbs so that no food be wasted.
**Narrator:** The people ate and were filled. Then the disciples gathered up the crumbs, which filled several baskets. *(Disciples take wastebaskets and pretend to fill them.)*
**Narrator:** When the people saw that more food was left over then they originally had, they began to shout.
**People:** Give us Jesus for our king! *(Repeat.)*
**Narrator:** But Jesus knew he could not be their king. It was not the plan of God the Father. So without their notice, he slipped away. *(Jesus leaves the room.)*

*End*

# PLAY 8

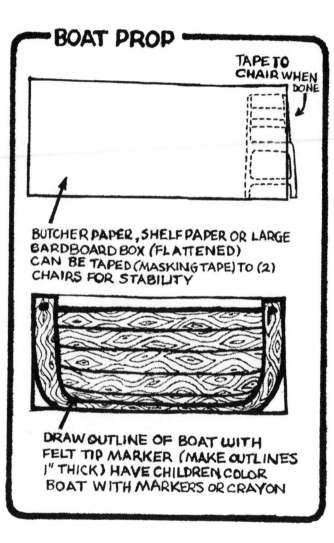

**BOAT PROP**

TAPE TO CHAIR WHEN DONE

BUTCHER PAPER, SHELF PAPER OR LARGE BARDBOARD BOX (FLATTENED) CAN BE TAPED (MASKING TAPE) TO (2) CHAIRS FOR STABILITY

DRAW OUTLINE OF BOAT WITH FELT TIP MARKER (MAKE OUTLINES 1" THICK) HAVE CHILDREN COLOR BOAT WITH MARKERS OR CRAYON

## Props and Production Notes:

**Boat.** See Production Notes, etc. on Jesus Calms the Storm for suggestions for boat, wave action, wind, etc.
Peter simulates sinking in water by slowly bending his knees to the floor. (For Peter choose the most dramatic, imaginative boy in class. You may get real ham!)

## Songs and Music:

"Help My Unbelief" Record album—SEASONS
"Peter" (Come to me over the water, Peter) Album—I HAVE THE SECRET by Medical Mission Sisters.

ter

# Script

## Characters

**Jesus**
**Disciples**

**Time:** Late evening

**Scene:** Disciples on boat crossing sea. *(See Production Notes, etc.)*

**Narrator:** It is growing dark. The disciples are in a boat. The wind blows, waves are high and boat rocks dangerously. They are frightened. They see a form walking toward them on the water.

**Peter:** Look! A ghost! *(pointing)* It's walking on water! *(All turn to look.) (Jesus walks slowly toward them.)*

**Matthew:** No that isn't a ghost. it's Jesus.

**Jesus** *(Stops walking):* Take courage. It is I. Do not be afraid.

**Peter:** Lord if it is you, let me come to you.

**Jesus:** Come, Peter. *(Peter climbs out of a boat and walks a few steps. Then slowly sinks to his knees looking frightened.)*

**Peter:** Jesus, save me! *(Kneels with arms outstretched to Jesus.)*

**Jesus** *(Walking over to Peter, grasps his arms and raises him to his feet)* O, you of little faith. Why did you doubt me? *(Waves and wind stop.) (Jesus and Peter walk together and climb into the boat.)*

**Disciples:** Jesus, You are truly the son of God! *(Repeat.)*

*End*

# PLAY 9

## Jesus Heals the Blind

### LUKE 19:35-43

### Play Season:

Use to illustrate compassion of Jesus for the handicapped. Also that we should call on the name of Jesus for mercy in our difficulties, as the blind man did. General use.

### Props and Production Notes:

Street Scene. No props needed. Corner of classroom or aisle.

### Songs and Music:

The Joy of the Lord is my Strength Sing Praise—from Album HI GOD, by Rev. Carey Landry and Carol Jean Kinghorn—North American Liturgy Resources
Praise to the Lord the Almighty the King of Creation—*Catholic Hymnal,* Student Ed. Benzinger.

Man

# Script

## Characters

**Jesus**
**Blind Man**
**Friend**
**Disciples (2 or 3)**
**Crowd of People**

**Time:** Early in the day.

**Scene:** On the road near Jericho. Blind man sits at the roadside A friend stands near him.

**Narrator:** Jesus and his disciples are on the way to Jericho. A crowd of people have joined his group as he walks along. They have heard of his miracles and are anxious to follow him. A blind beggar sits near the road and his friend stands by him. The crowd is noisy. All seem to talk at once.

**Blind Man** *(To friend):* What is happening? I hear voices.

**Friend:** A crowd of people are following Jesus of Nazareth.

**Blind Man:** Jesus, Son of David, have mercy on me! *(Louder)* Jesus, Son of David, have mercy on me!

**Man in Crowd:** Be quiet! Stop that yelling.

**Blind Man:** Jesus, son of David, have mercy!

**Jesus** *(Stops walking):* Who calls my name?

**Man in Crowd:** Only an old, blind beggar.

**Jesus:** Bring him to me. *(They help the beggar to Jesus.)*

**Jesus:** What would you have me do for you?

**Blind Man:** Please, Jesus, that I may see.

**Jesus** *(Touching the man's eyelids):* Receive your sight. Your faith has saved you.

**Blind Man** *(Opening his eyes):* I can see! *(Shouts)* I can see! Thank you Jesus, thank you. *(He follows the crowd praising Jesus.)*

*End*

# PLAY 10

## The Good Samarita
### LUKE 10:25-37

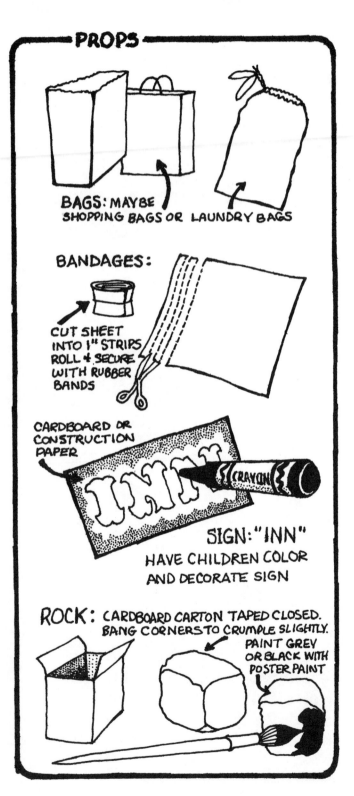

PROPS

BAGS: MAYBE SHOPPING BAGS OR LAUNDRY BAGS

BANDAGES:

CUT SHEET INTO 1" STRIPS ROLL & SECURE WITH RUBBER BANDS

CARDBOARD OR CONSTRUCTION PAPER

CRAYON

SIGN: "INN"
HAVE CHILDREN COLOR AND DECORATE SIGN

ROCK: CARDBOARD CARTON TAPED CLOSED. BANG CORNERS TO CRUMPLE SLIGHTLY. PAINT GREY OR BLACK WITH POSTER PAINT

## Play Season:

Following a discussion on loving our neighbor, who, as Jesus tells us, is everyone on earth. A good opportunity to discuss all prejudices, including those of race, creed and color. Point out that the Jewish man and the Samaritan were not of the same religion. This play has been a top favorite with the children and may be used at any time.

## Props and Production Notes:

**Scene I. Jewish man, Good Samaritan and Travelers carry packs slung over their backs.** May be shopping bags or other cloth bags. Samaritan's pack must have bandage material (strips of old sheets, or any white cloth) and money (paper cut to size).
**Rock.** A desk, large cardboard carton, etc.
**Scene II At Inn.** A closet or classroom door may be used as door to inn. Innkeeper stands on other side of door. *A sign* "INN" may be pasted on door.

WAGON: (IF AVAILABLE) MAY BE USED AS DONKEY

In this scene the Samaritan helps Jewish man to walk to the inn. Too difficult to construct a mobile donkey as mentioned in bible story.

## Songs and Music:

Who is My Neighbor, Album: SEASONS, by Medical Mission Sisters.
A New Commandment, Album: HAND IN HAND, by Joe Wise, World Library of Sacred Music.

**Note:**
One delightfully imaginative teacher using this play fashioned a donkey from the game Pin the Tail on the Donkey, taped to the side of a small wagon. She changed a few lines of the script to conform. I suppose a donkey could be fashioned of cardboard and used in this manner but I hesitated to include this because of detailed instruction required. Use your own judgement!

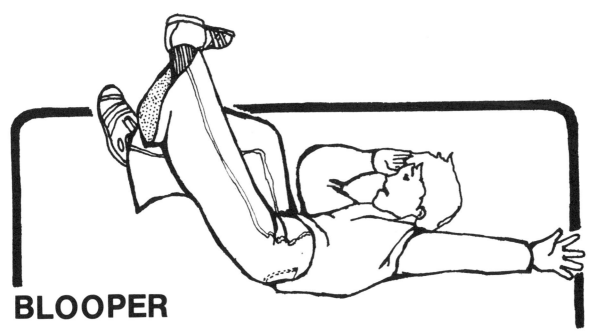

# BLOOPER

On one occasion when producing The Good Samaritan, the injured Jewish man suffered severely. He rolled around in such agony, moaning so realistically that we had to stop the play to make sure he had not been injured in the scuffle. What a "ham."

# PLAY 10

## The Good Samaritan
### LUKE 10:25-37

## Script

### Characters

Jewish Man
Robbers (2)
First Traveler
Second Traveler
Samaritan
Innkeeper

**Scene:** Along the road from Jerusalem to Jericho.

**Narrator:** Jesus often spoke to the people in parables. A parable is a little story used to explain a lesson or teaching. In this way Jesus explained things so people could understand. One day a young man asked Jesus, "Who is my neighbor?" Jesus told him the story of the Good Samaritan.

**Jewish Man** (*Walks along with a pack on his back, talking to himself):* When I sell my goods, I'll buy gifts for my family.

**Robbers** (*Jumping out from behind a rock):* Give us that pack.

**Jewish Man:** No, I must sell this to get money for my family.

**Robbers** (*Struggling for the pack. Jewish man tries to hang on to it):* If you don't give it to us, we will beat you. (*Man still*

holds on. *Robbers pretend to beat him with their fists.)*

**Jewish Man** *(Falls down, moans and lies still.)*

**Robbers:** Let's run. Someone is coming. *(They run off with pack.)*

**First Traveler** *(Walks over to injured man and looks at him):* Poor man! Robbers must have beat him. But I can't help him. I'm in a hurry. *(walks off.)*

**Second Traveler** *(Walks over, looks at injured man):* He needs help, but he is not of my religion. *(He walks away.)*

**Samaritan** *(Passing by, notices the man, walks over to him and kneels down beside him):* Poor fellow, are you badly hurt?

**Jewish Man** *Groans :* I don't think so. If you will help me up, I will try to walk.

**Samaritan:** First let me take care of your wounds. *(Opens his own pack and takes out bandages. Ties one around man's head and another around his arm. Then helps the man to his feet.)*

**Jewish Man:** Thank you, sir. You are very kind. *(He staggers.)*

**Samaritan:** I don't think you are able to go far. Over there is an inn. I will take you there. *(They walk to inn, Samaritan helping the man who is limping badly.)*

**Scene II**

**Samaritan** *(Knocking on inn door.) (See Production Notes, etc.):* Please let us in.

**Innkeeper** *(Opens door):* Yes! *(Looking at man):* What happened to him?

**Samaritan:** Robbers beat and robbed him. Will you take care of him 'till I return tomorrow?

**Inn Keeper:** Yes, I will take care of him. Come in.

**Samaritan:** Thank you. *(Reaches into his pack and hands money to innkeeper.)* Here's some money. If it is not enough, I'll give you more when I return.

**Narrator:** Jesus asked the young man, "Which do you think was a neighbor to the injured man?" *(to class):* Which do you think?

**Class:** The one who helped him.

**Narrator:** You are right. Jesus then told the young man to help anyone who needs help, because everyone is our neighbor.

End

# PLAY II

## Jesus Brings Daught

**MARK 5:21**

## PROPS:

## Play Season:

An appropriate time to discuss our own resurrection. Also to discuss our spiritual resurrection when we receive Sacraments.

## Props and Production Notes:

**Scene I. Street Scene.** No props.
**Scene II.** Room in Jairus' house. **Chairs** may be used to outline room, or square roped off with heavy cord attached to five chairs (corners), or a chalk outline on the floor. Daughter's bed may be two or three chairs placed side by side. Other furnishings, if available.

## Songs and Music:

Let There be Peace, from Album SEASONS by Medical Mission Sisters (Avant Garde AVS 126).
Take my Hand Precious Lord, from *Reader's Digest Songbook of Faith and Joy.*

# of Jairus To Life

## Script

### (2 Scenes)

## Characters

Jesus
Peter
James
John
Jairus
Jairus' Wife
Jairus' Daughter
Servant
Mourners

### Scene I

**Time:** Late in day.

**Setting:** A street scene.

**Narrator:** Jesus and his disciples walk slowly along a road. A man named Jairus rushes up to them.

**Jairus** *(Taking Jesus by the arm):* Jesus, please hurry to my home. My little daughter is dying. Just lay your hands on her.

**Servant** *(Runs up excitedly to Jairus and tugs at his sleeve):* Master, do not bother Jesus now. Your daughter is dead.

**Jairus** *(Covering his face with his hands):* My poor child.

**Jesus** *(Puts arm over Jairus' shoulder):* Do not be afraid. Come we will go to your house. Have faith.

### Scene II

**Setting:** Home of Jairus. Mourners stand outside the door weeping.

**Jesus** *(To mourners):* Why do you weep? The girl is asleep, not dead. *(Mourners stop weeping and look questioningly at Jesus.)*

**Mourner** *(To another):* How can he say that? The child has been dead for hours.

**Jesus** *(To Jairus):* Take me to the child. *(Jesus, the disciples and Jairus enter the room. Jairus' wife stands weeping beside the bed on which the child lies, eyes closed, hands folded on chest.)*

**Jesus** *(To Jairus' wife):* Stop crying. She is only sleeping. *(Jairus' wife stops, looks at Jesus questioningly.)*

**Jesus** *(Taking child's hand):* Girl, I say to you, arise.

**Girl** *(Opens her eyes, looks around and sits):* Yes, Jesus. *(All look shocked, then happy. Jairus and wife embrace their daughter.)*

**Jesus:** Tell no one of this. *(To Jairus):* Let there be peace in your dwelling.

End

# PLAY 12

## The Prodigal Son
### LUKE 15:11-24

## Play Season:

Especially good for use in preparation for reception of the sacrament of Penance. Also to make comparison of God, our own loving and forgiving Father and the loving, forgiving father of the Prodigal Son.

## Props and Production Notes:

**Scenes I & III. Room in Father's house.** Chairs may be used to outline room, or square roped off with cord attached to five chairs. Chairs used to form corners plus doorway. A few small pieces of furniture, if available. Money—newspaper cut to size.
**Ring** from Father's hand. A large, ornate costume jewelry ring is best.
**Scene II.** Door to Farmer's house. A closet or classroom door. Farmer stands on other side of door.

## Songs and Music:

Loving Father Ever Waiting, *People's Mass Book.* 3rd Ed. (Voice Book.)
Ballad of the Prodigal Son, Album: I KNOW A SECRET. Medical Mission Sisters, AVS-105.

## BLOOPER

While presenting The Prodigal Son, the son wouldn't accept the "sissy" ring. He demanded a wristwatch!

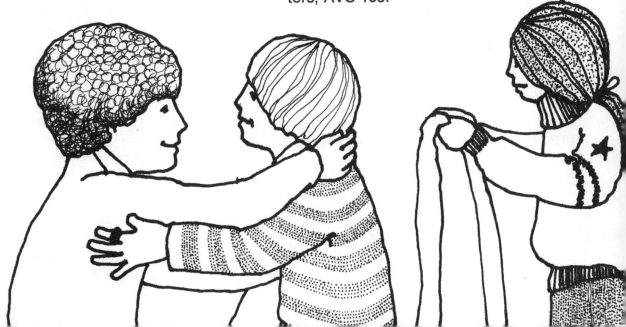

# Script

## Characters
Father
Son
Farmer
Servant

### Scene I

**Scene:** Room in father's house. *(See Production Notes, etc.)*

**Narrator:** Jesus often spoke to the people in parables. A parable is a story used to explain a lesson or teaching. Jesus told this parable. A rich man has two sons. The youngest son wants to leave home. The father is sad.

**Son:** Father, will you give me my share of your property?

**Father:** Why do you need so much money, son?

**Son:** I want to go out into the world and have fun. Here *(gestures with hands)* there's no fun, just boring work.

**Father:** All right, son, if you wish. *(Reaches in his pocket and gives his son a handful of bills.)*

**Son** *(Takes money):* Good-bye, Father. *(Walks off smiling and dancing.) (Father sadly watches him go.)*

**Narrator:** The son has a great time, partying, drinking and dancing with his new friends. But, after his money is gone, they all leave him. He is alone and hungry

### Scene II

**Scene:** At door of farmer's house.

**Son:** I'll ask this farmer if he will give me work and food. *(Knocks on door. Farmer opens door.)*

**Farmer** *(Opens door):* Yes? What do you want?

**Son:** Will you please give me work and food? I am hungry.

**Farmer:** You can take care of my pigs. You can eat the food that they eat. *(He closes door.)*

**Son** *(Sits down on ground):* Why did I ever leave home? My father loved me. If I go home, will he forgive me? I don't deserve his love. Perhaps he will chase me away. No, not if he loves me. I don't deserve his love. But I'll go home.

### Scene III

**Scene:** Father's house. Father stands in doorway.

**Father** *(Sees the son returning. Runs to meet him and embraces him):* My son, thank God, you have come home.

**Son:** Yes Father, Can you forgive me? Will you let me work as your servant? I don't deserve to be your son.

**Father:** I am happy you have come home, my son. *(Calls servant)*

*Servant enters.*

**Father** Get my best cloak and put it around him.

*Father to son:* Here's a gold ring for your finger. *(Removes his ring and gives it to son.)*

**Son:** Father, I will never leave you again.

**Father:** We will prepare a banquet to celebrate your homecoming.

End.

# PLAY 13

## The Last Supper

LUKE 22:14-21
MATTHEW 26:20-35

### Play Season:

Use in preparation for Holy Week, also for first Holy Communion. Stress that Jesus chose to institute the Holy Eucharist in order that he might remain with us after his death for when we receive him in Holy Communion he comes to live in our bodies.

### Props and Production Notes:

**Long table** or several small tables together, or long strip of white shelf paper stretched on floor. Children sit around it picnic style.
Jesus sits at center of table. John next to Jesus, and Peter beside John. Judas sits beside Peter, etc. Disciples' names should be assigned previous to seating.
**Paper cup and plate at each place.**
**Large glass** (chalice shaped, if possible) for Jesus.
**Plate of bread or rolls.**
**Wine is a fruit drink.**

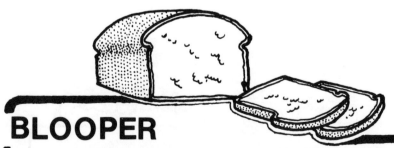

## BLOOPER

During The Last Supper presentation, a little girl looking sad and sympathetic inquired, "Did Jesus always have to eat his bread without butter?" When told he did, she ate hers silently.

# Script

## Characters

Jesus
Disciples (12)
Friends (If desired)

**Time:** Evening of Holy Thursday

**Scene:** Large dining hall in Jerusalem. Everyone is seated at the table. *(See Production Notes, etc.)*

**Narrator:** It is the Jewish feast celebrating the freedom of the Jews from slavery. Jesus has asked the disciples to eat the Passover meal with him. He knows he is about to be betrayed to his enemies and wants to prepare them for his death.

**Jesus:** I have greatly wished to share this meal with you before I leave you.

**Peter:** It is good to celebrate this Passover meal with you, Jesus, but why do you look so sad?

**Jesus:** One who will betray me is at this table. *(Disciples look at one another, then at Jesus.)*

**Disciples:** Is it I, Master? Is it I? *(Then they quietly await Jesus' reply.)*

**Judas:** Is it I, Master?

**Jesus** *(Looks at Judas for a few seconds in silence. All others also look at Judas):* You have said it. *(Judas leaves the room.)*

**Disciples** *(Looking puzzled at one another):* What was that all about?

**Jesus:** If you had really known me, you would have understood.

**Narrator:** Jesus takes bread, blesses it, breaks it and gives a piece to each disciple. *(Cue to Jesus.)*

**Jesus:** Take this and eat. This is my body which is being given for you. Do this in remembrance of me.

**Narrator:** Then Jesus takes the cup of wine and raises it, looking up to heaven. *(Cue to Jesus.)*

**Jesus:** This is my blood which shall be shed for you. Drink it. It will be shed for the forgiveness of sins. *(Disciples drink.)*

**Jesus:** In a little while I will leave you.

**Peter:** Jesus, wherever you go, I will go with you.

**Jesus:** Where I go now you cannot follow, but you will later.

**Peter:** Master, I will lay down my life for you.

**Jesus:** Peter! Peter! Before the cock crows you will disown me three times. *(Peter, looking sad, bows his head.)*

**All** (Sing Hymn): Father, Thy Will Be Done, Rec. KNOCK, KNOCK, Medical Mission Sisters.

**Jesus:** Love one another and keep My Commandments. I will be with you. Come! *(Jesus rises from the table)* I must go to the garden to pray to the Father. *(All exit quietly.)*

*End.*

# PLAY IT — The Resurrection
## MARK 16:1-7
## JOHN 20:1-19

**COSTUMES**

CUT SHEET IN HALF
FOLD OVER +
CUT NECK-
HOLE

NOTE: MAKE ROBE
WHITE FOR
JESUS
CAN MAKE AND
COLOR (WITH
STRIPES OR
FLOWERS)
FOR ANGEL

FOR ANGEL A HALO CAN
BE MADE WITH COAT
HANGER —
STRAIGHTEN HANGER
THEN TWIST INTO
SHAPE SHOWN AT LEFT
FIT TO HEAD OF ANGEL

## Play Season:

Especially for Easter Season. By keeping his promise to rise from the dead, Jesus proved to mankind that he was the son of God.

## Props and Production:

**A closet may be used as tomb.** The door slightly ajar, substituting for the heavy stone door. Angel may stand just on other side of door. If no closet is available, Angel may stand or sit just outside the classroom door.
**Angel may wear white robe.** See Note following Play 1 Angels Announce Jesus' Birth, etc.
Occasionally it is best to select a girl for the angel. Some boys are embarrassed to wear a robe (dress).

## Songs and Music:

Jesus Christ is Risen Today, from *People's Mass Book,* Sunday and Holyday Edition. 3rd Ed. No. 30.
Run, Come, See II, from Album RUN, COME, SEE F.E.L. Record Release S-272 Stereo.

When asked to wear a white robe as an angel, one little boy objected to the "dress." He asked, "When men wore long hair and dresses, how could they tell them from the girls?" A sharp little girl answered quickly, "The same way you can tell the girls with short hair and pants from the boys." She didn't elaborate; we were afraid to pursue the subject.

esus

# Script

## Characters

**Jesus**
**Mary of Magdala**
**Mary of James**
**Young Man (Angel)**
**Disciples**

**Time:** Early Easter morning
**Scene:** Tomb of Jesus
**Narrator:** It is early morning of Easter Sunday. The two Marys are walking along the road. They are going to visit the place where Jesus is buried. They loved him very much and miss him. They are sad. As they come near Jesus' tomb they can hardly believe their eyes. The big stone that had covered the opening to the grave has been pushed aside.
**Mary of Magda:** Look! The tomb is open! *(They reach the tomb and look inside.)*
**Narrator:** A young man is sitting near the stone. He smiles at them. This person is called an Angel, because he is a messenger from God.
**Angel:** Do not be afraid. I know you are looking for Jesus. He is not here. He has risen as he said he would. Go quickly and tell his Disciples that Jesus is alive. *(The two Marys start to hurry away but stop suddenly. They see a man coming.)*
**Mary of James:** Who is that man?
**Mary of Magda:** I do not know but we must hurry.
**Narrator:** They do not recognize him but the man is Jesus. As he comes near he speaks to them.
**Jesus:** Peace be with you.
**Narrator:** The two Marys then recognize Jesus and fall to their knees. They are so happy to see him they wrap their arms around his feet. *(Cue to Marys.)*
**Two Marys:** Master, you have come back to us. *(They smile up at Jesus.)*
**Jesus** *(Gently touching their heads):* Don't cling to me. Go tell the others I will meet them in Galilee. *(The Marys rise to their feet. Smiling they hurry away shouting.)*
**Two Marys:** Jesus lives! Jesus Lives! He is risen from the dead.

End

# PLAY 15

## Jesus Is Found In T

Luke 2:41-52

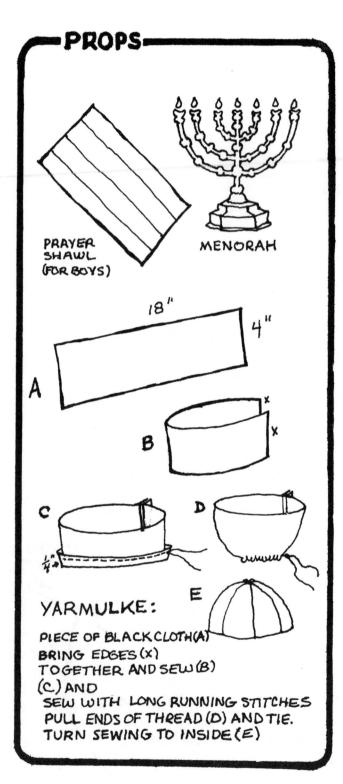

PRAYER SHAWL (FOR BOYS)

MENORAH

18"

4"

A

B

C

D

E

YARMULKE:

PIECE OF BLACK CLOTH (A)
BRING EDGES (X)
TOGETHER AND SEW (B)
(C) AND
SEW WITH LONG RUNNING STITCHES
PULL ENDS OF THREAD (D) AND TIE.
TURN SEWING TO INSIDE (E)

## Play Season:

For use at any time during the year.

## Props and Production Notes:

Mark off area to be designated as room in Temple by Narrator. **Furnishings. Two chairs** placed side by side for Teachers. **Small table with a Menorah,** or other candle holder with candles. Boys may wear **prayer shawls.** Plain colored or striped (not flowered) scarves, or strips of material. Boys' woolen scarves are ideal. Yarmulkes also may be worn by the boys. Narrator explains the small, black skullcap called a yarmulke. Simple ones can be made easily. Take a strip of black cloth, approximately 4″ x 18″. Join the 4 inch ends (x's) by sewing together. Then sew all the way around one 18″ length of cloth, about ¼″ from the edge with long, running stitches. Gather by pulling thread tightly. This forms a small cap. Turn stitched edges inside to wear.

**Note:** Prayer shawls and yarmulke are not necessary to the play, but do add a Jewish note.

# Temple

## Songs and Music:

Opening Scene—Eli, Eli. Many recordings available. Album Jan Peerce Sings Hebrew Melodies in Hebrew. Excellent. Also words and music in English and Hebrew in volume 95 *World Famous Songs*—Published by Robbins Music Corp.

For Finale: I've Heard His Word, from Album *Celebrate—Songs of Early Childhood* by Sadlier. Or, Faith of Our Fathers—Many recordings, or song books.

## BLOOPER

In the temple scene of Jesus Is Found in the Temple, a boy was disappointed that he couldn't wear the "beanie" he had brought from home as a yarmulke. The gyro on top wasn't exactly kosher.

# PLAY 15

## Jesus Is Found In T

Luke 2:41-52

## Script

### Characters

**Jesus**
**Mary**
**Joseph**

**Teachers (2)**
**Worshippers**—Any number

**Scene:** Room in the Temple *(See Production Notes, etc.)*

**Background Music:** Eli, Eli *(Recording, Played softly.)*

**Narrator:** Jesus is now 12 years old and has accompanied his mother Mary and Joseph to the Temple to celebrate the Jewish feast of Passover. Jesus sits at the feet of the teachers. Men are seated in a group on the floor behind Jesus. Women sit behind men. Men wear prayer shawls over their shoulders and yarmulkes on their heads. The yarmulke is worn by Jewish men to indicate they honor God and are devout Jews. *(Music stops.)*

**Teacher:** Now, my dear people, our Feast of Passover has ended. You may return to your homes. Shalom!

**Jesus** *(Looking up to teachers):* Will you please teach me more? *(Teachers and Jesus remain seated. Others rise to go.)*

**Narrator:** Men remove their prayer shawls, fold them and place them on the table. They leave the temple in a group, followed by the women in another group. No one has noticed that Jesus is not with them. *(They walk a distance from the Temple.)*

**Joseph** *(Turning, calls to Mary):* Mary, is Jesus with you?

# Temple

**Mary:** No Joseph, I thought he was with you. *(Groups stop walking.)*

**Joseph** *(To men in group):* Have you seen Jesus?

**Men:** Not since we left the Temple.

**Mary** *(To women):* Have you seen Jesus since we left the Temple?

**Women:** No, Mary.

**Joseph:** Come, Mary, we have walked a long way, but we must go back and find him. *(They turn back. Groups continue and exit.)*

**Narrator:** Mary and Joseph return to Jerusalem and enter the Temple. Jesus is seated on the floor, listening attentively to teachers. *(Mary and Joseph walk toward Jesus. Jesus rises to his feet.)*

**Teacher** *(Looking at Joseph):* We have been amazed at his wisdom. He has studied his lessons well.

**Mary** *(to Jesus):* Son, why have you done this to us?

**Joseph:** We were so worried. We thought you were lost.

**Jesus:** Why have you worried? Didn't you know I must be about my Father's business? This is my Father's house.

**Joseph** *(To Mary):* Mary, do you understand his words?

**Mary:** No, Joseph, they puzzle me. But he is the son of God.

**Jesus** *(To Teachers):* Shalom, my teachers. *(Jesus removes the prayer shawl and places it on the table. He leaves the Temple with Mary and Joseph.)*

**Narrator:** Jesus, with Mary and Joseph returned to their home in Nazareth. There, the bible tells us, he grew in age, in wisdom and in grace.

End

### He's Got The Whole World In His Hands

Several recordings: Anita Bryant's is one of the best. Also by Mahalia Jackson, et al.
Music and words in *Family Songbook of Faith and Joy*—Reader's Digest.
We used this song with gestures:
At words "hands"—hands are outstretched, palms up.
At words "world"—arms raised in circle, fingertips touching.
At words "brothers and sisters"—each child points to another boy and girl.
At words "little baby"—arms in cradling position, and sway from waist.
At words "everybody here"—sweeping arms motion to indicate all present.

*****

### Kumbaya

Several recordings. One Album—The Impossible Dream, by Living Voices, is one of the best. Also music and words in Reader's Digest Songbook, etc. Simple words and good rythm for clapping.

*****

### Amen

Several recordings. Album ORANGE BLOSSOM SPECIAL, by Johnny Cash, has good recording, but some other songs on record are not suitable for children. Also in Reader's Digest Songbook. Children love to join in the vigorous Amen, clap hands in rhythm.

*****

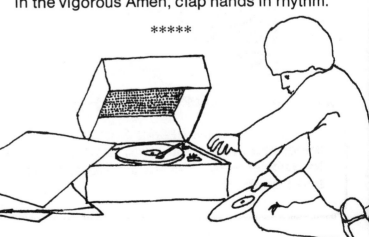

# OVED BY CHILDREN

**Other Songs Most Loved By Children**

**Little Drummer Boy**

**A Disneyland Album. Children enjoy singing along on the Rumpa, Pum, Pum. Other good songs on the album.**

\* \* \* \* \*

**Other Albums we have used:**

HAND IN HAND, by Joe Wise
COME ALIVE AT CHRISTMAS, by The Sacred Heart Sisters
RUN, COME, SEE, by Robert Blue
JOY IS LIKE THE RAIN, by Medical Mission Sisters
SONGS FOR YOUNG CHILDREN—Paulist/Newman Press
HI GOD!—North American Liturgy Resources

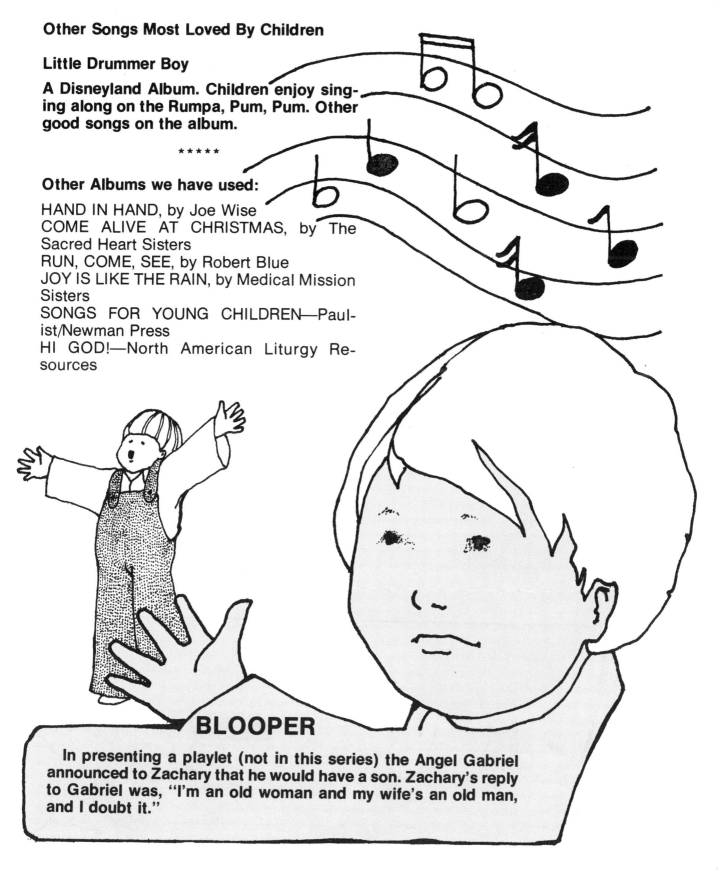

## BLOOPER

In presenting a playlet (not in this series) the Angel Gabriel announced to Zachary that he would have a son. Zachary's reply to Gabriel was, "I'm an old woman and my wife's an old man, and I doubt it."

# If they loved the Jesus Plays, They will love The Parables!

## THE PARABLES

(Sound-filmstrip series)

Add 9 of Jesus' favorite parables to your religion class with ease.

Carefully scripted for girls and boys in the primary grades. Portrayed in full color photography or captivating, cartoon-style, original art.

Angry factory workers protest equal wages paid to handicapped employees in 'The Toy Factory' (The Vineyard Workers) from Set 1.

The boy from across the street is the only one to lend a hand in 'Franklin' (The Good Samaritan) from Set 2.

Contemporary story lines re-cast Jesus' message in fresh, vivid classroom presentations of 4 to 7 minutes each.

Three stories to each sound-filmstrip set retell the following parables:

### Primary Set 1
The Unjust Steward
The Vineyard Workers
Rich Man and Lazarus

### Primary Set 2
Lamp Under a Bushel
Good Shepherd
Good Samaritan

### Primary Set 3
The Great Banquet
The Dragnet
The Two Sons

## Your handy ordering guide

Each set contains 1 filmstrip, complete guide for three stories on filmstrip, and your choice of record or cassette.

All three sets .................... ONLY $59.85
Each set separately .............. ONLY $19.95
(Cassettes $1.00 per set)

Mail Order today To:

## TWENTY-THIRD PUBLICATIONS
P.O. Box 180
West Mystic, Ct. 06388
(Make sure to include complete mailing address)